Horst Bielfeld

W9-BDJ-824

Guinea Pigs

Horst Bielfeld

Guinea Pigs

Everything about Purchase, Care,
Nutrition, and Diseases

With 17 Color Photographs by Outstanding Animal
Photographers and 35 Drawings by Fritz W. Köhler

Translated by Helgard Niewisch, D.V.M.

Barron's
New York/London/Toronto/Sydney

First English language edition published in 1983 by
Barron's Educational Series, Inc.
© 1977 by Gräfe and Unzer GmbH, Munich,
West Germany.

The title of the German book is *Meerschweinchen.*

All inquiries should be addressed to:
Barron's Educational Series, Inc.
250 Wireless Boulevard
Hauppauge, New York 11788

Library of Congress Catalog Card No. 83-2735
International Standard Book No. 0-8120-2629-2

Library of Congress Cataloging in Publication Data

Bielfeld, Horst.
    Guinea pigs.

    Translation of: *Meerschweinchen.*
    Bibliography: p. 67.
    Includes index.
    Summary: Discusses guinea pig breeds and
breeding, care and feeding, anatomy, behavior, and
diseases.
    1. Guinea pigs as pets. [1. Guinea pigs]
I. Köhler, Fritz W., ill. II. Title.
SF459.G9B5313 1983   636'.93234   83-2735
ISBN 0-8120-2629-2

Front cover: A beautifully marked English Checked
    guinea pig.
Inside front cover: Red and white Abyssinian
    guinea pig.
Inside back cover: A family of multicolored
    Checked guinea pigs.

Cover design: Heinz Kraxenberger, Munich

Photographs
Bielfeld: Front cover, pages 53, 54, 64 (above left,
    above right, below right), inside back cover
Coleman/Reinhard: page 28
Dr. Jesse: Inside front cover
Prenzel: page 9
Reinhard: page 63
Schmidecker: pages 10, 27, 64 (below left), back
    cover (below left)

901   977   15 14 13 12 11 10

Contents

Contents

Preface

My first encounter with guinea pigs came shortly before World War II, when I was a small boy. At the time I lived with my parents in the city of Danzig (Poland) in an apartment where the landlord did not allow pets, and I always looked forward to visits with my cousins in the country because they were allowed to keep guinea pigs. Their pets were handsome, tricolored, smooth-haired animals. I was allowed to play with them, and I was also entrusted with the daily care of some of these animals for the duration of my stay. It meant a lot to me as a small boy to care for them myself. I learned the meaning of responsibility because it was up to me to feed the animals, keep their cages clean, and comb and brush them. This kind of contact with a good-natured, soft, and furry pet fosters a love for animals in young people. Even though I later owned a canary and a Greek land turtle, I am convinced that my early childhood experience with guinea pigs was primarily responsible for the special relationship I have developed with animals.

My later childhood and youth were spent near the city of Hamburg in West Germany. There, my parents had a large yard, and I finally had the chance to keep all kinds of pets. At that time I realized that my love for animals would determine my life's work. I began to photograph animals and write about them. As an adult, I have traveled to a number of countries and continents and have come to know all kinds of different animals.

I did not keep a guinea pig again, however, until my oldest son was five years old. This was a young male that we named Maximilian. The children loved him dearly. Indeed, our youngest daughter embraced him so passionately one day that the delicate animal

At about five years old children can start learning to care for a guinea pig themselves.

did not survive her demonstration of affection. That was an important, if bitter, lesson for us all. Guinea pigs enjoy being petted and cuddled, and children can also be allowed to carry them around. But two- and three-year-olds should always have adult supervision when they handle their pets. Youngsters often do not know their own strength; and where dogs

Birgit and her young checked guinea pig. ▷
He already feels at home in the hands of his
young owner.

and cats will fight back by biting and scratching if they are squeezed too hard, guinea pigs remain passive. I therefore feel that children should be at least five years old before they are given guinea pigs. At that age they can understand how to treat such an animal properly, and they are able to care for and feed him themselves, though supervision by parents or older siblings may sometimes be necessary. Our replacement for Maximilian, who had literally been loved to death, was Maja, a tricolored, smooth-haired female. Maja was a lively and affectionate animal and possessed of an intelligence far superior to anything we would have expected in a guinea pig. In the section "Sensory Capacities and Ability to Learn" I describe some experiments we performed primarily with her. These were not so much scientific experiments as they were examples of meaningful play, and both the guinea pig and our children learned a lot from them.

We brought our first guinea pig home twelve years ago, and we have had six more since then, sometimes keeping two or three at a time. We have had enjoyable and exciting experiences with all of them. Balduin once ran into a thicket of rose bushes bordering on a heavily traveled road. Our efforts to extract him resembled a jungle expedition, but our scratches and torn clothes were soon forgotten, for we had accomplished our mission: Balduin had been rescued, safe and sound. The guinea pig that now has the run of our home is called Korina. She is my little daughter's pride and joy.

Guinea pigs are often misrepresented as stupid and uninteresting animals. Anyone who observes them and tries to understand them will soon see that this is not the case. In this "pet owner's guide for the younger generation," you will learn to understand your guinea pig better. You will also learn everything you need to know about purchase, care, diet, and diseases. This knowledge is essential to insure that your pet has a long, healthy life. It is equally important that you give him a lot of attention, for his instincts and sensory capacities need constant challenge. Living in the wild, a guinea pig has to use all of his innate abilities to survive. He has to elude a large number of enemies and find food and shelter. When we play with him, we challenge him to perform substitute activities and so enable him to live at least somewhat in keeping with the nature of his species. Your pet will respond eagerly and gratefully, and you will derive a great deal of pleasure from this contact with your pet.

Horst Bielfeld

8

◁ A tricolored English checked guinea pig. His posture indicates alert attention.

From Wild Animal to Pet

Wild Guinea Pigs and Their Relatives

Guinea pigs (or cavies) belong to the superfamily Cavioidae, which also includes the Patagonian cavy or mara and the capybara. Maras can be as long as 30 inches (70 cm) and weigh 35 pounds (16 kg).* Capybaras grow to as much as 4½ feet (130 cm) in length, can weigh upwards of 100 pounds (50 kg), and are the largest known rodents. Despite the difference in size between the capybara and the wild guinea pig, which weighs only about 2 pounds (1 kg) and is 8 to 14 inches (22–35 cm) in length, it is obvious that they are related. They both have a relatively large head and a very short tail or none at all. They have four toes on their front feet and only three on the hind. The hind toes have broad,

*Comparable metric measurements are given in parentheses throughout the book.

hoof-type nails. Both species walk on their toes and have a similar gait.

In the subfamily Caviinae are the genera *Cavia* (the true cavies), *Kerodon* (rock cavy), and *Galea* and *Microcavia* (mountain, marsh, and pampas cavies). Of these genera we are primarily interested in the *Cavia* because the ancestors of our domestic guinea pigs belong to it.

Domestic Animal of the South American Indians

The *Cavia aperea* is the most widespread species in South America, occurring there in the northern, western, and southeastern parts of that immense continent. The cavy that lives in the western regions (*Cavia aperea tschudii*) is generally considered to be the wild ancestor of our guinea pig. The reports of the early explorers suggest that the Indians in other parts of South and Central America kept other breeds of this same species.

In the wild, guinea pigs move on well-worn paths in single file. This maintains close contact between one animal and another.

11

From Wild Animal to Pet

The Mountain Cavy

This guinea pig is also called the Tschudi cavy after the Swiss zoologist Tschudi. It lives in northern Chile and southern Peru and is a mountain animal inhabiting—like the European marmot—vegetated slopes at 13,000 feet (4,000 m) and above. This guinea pig digs dens in the ground, but it prefers to move into dens abandoned by other animals. Like all cavies, it is active during daylight hours. The animals of one clan stay close together in groups of as few as four or as many as twenty. They forage together, forming a labyrinth of tunnel-like paths in the tall grass. These animals are agile and quick, and they warn each other of danger by whistling or squeaking. At this warning signal, they all take flight and hide themselves in thickets or their dens. Even only a few hours after birth the young are so agile and quick that they have an excellent chance of eluding their enemies. If they should be surprised by a predator, they will lie absolutely motionless and can often save themselves this way.

Lowland Cavies

Other *Aperea* breeds are lowland dwellers that inhabit grassy areas and underbrush. Some dig their own dens; others move into ones abandoned by other animals; and still others seek their shelter in dense grass and thickets. A few breeds that live in swamplands do not have any kind of dens at all. But as a rule, cavies prefer dry grassy areas and avoid the tropical forests of the Amazon River basin.

Other strains of the *Cavea, Galea,* and *Microcavia* genera live much as the *Aperea* strains do, using dens or hideouts in the grass or brush. They are all fast and agile runners in the underbrush, but they are not adept at climbing or jumping. One exception to this rule is the rock cavy or moko of the *Kerodon* genus. This cavy lives in rock crevices in the mountainous areas of southeastern Brazil. The moko can jump several yards, get about easily on rock cliffs, and climb trees to get juicy young leaves to eat.

The Ancient Incas Owned Guinea Pigs

Long before the discovery of America the South American Indians kept domestic guinea pigs. Archaeological excavations of Inca settlements and tombs have turned up guinea pig mummies, skeletons, and hair. We will probably never know exactly when and how the Indians of Panama domesticated guinea pigs, but it is reported that on their first journey through this part of Central America, Balboa and his men saw guinea pigs everywhere in the Indians' homes. The conquistadors with Pizarro, Almagro,

From Wild Animal to Pet

Quesada, Orellana, and Valdivia also found guinea pigs in all the Indian settlements, and when the Spaniards were short of food, they ate guinea pigs, just as the Indians did all the time. These conquerors were out to find gold, silver, and precious stones to bring back to Spain, and they had little space on their ships for these small, grey-brown animals. But the Spaniards must have taken some to Europe around 1540 because the Swiss zoologist Gessner described them as early as 1554. Some Inca tribes, like the Quetchua, for example, used the guinea pig not only for food but also as a sacrificial animal. The brown and white checked breeds were particularly favored as sacrifices for the sun god and as gifts placed in the tombs of the dead. Mummies of these animals show that domestication of the guinea pig in South America was highly advanced as early as 500 years ago.

How the Guinea Pig Came to Europe

It is uncertain whether any of the guinea pigs first brought to Europe by the Spanish around 1540 had offspring that survived. We do know, however, that guinea pigs were brought to Holland from Dutch Guiana about 1670.

Guinea pigs enjoy eating corn, a vegetable they find in the fields of their South American homeland.

The Dutch *Meerzwijn*

Dutch merchants found these cute, affectionate animals in Guiana and brought them home to the Netherlands as pets for their children. The guinea pigs tolerated the long voyage well, adapted readily to their environment, and multiplied rapidly. As early as 1680 guinea pigs bred in Holland were being sold to buyers in France and England. At first, they were very expensive, and only wealthy people could afford them as curiosities and as toys for their children. They later became popular pets in Holland, England, and Germany because they were so easy to keep and breed.

It is easy to see why the Dutch gave this little animal the name *meerzwijn* ("sea-pig"). It came from across the sea; it squeals like a pig; and both its chubby body and its gait resemble those of a small pig.

From Wild Animal to Pet

Why We Say "Guinea Pig"

Like Dutch, English calls this animal a kind of "pig," but where does the word "guinea" come from? One explanation has to do with money — the English coin known as a guinea. The first imported guinea pigs were very expensive, costing one guinea apiece. This is twenty-one shillings or slightly more than one pound sterling. "Guinea pig" thus meant "the little pig that costs a guinea."

Guinea Pigs in French and Spanish

In French the guinea pig is called *cobaye* or *cochon d'Inde,* which means "pig of India." This latter name derives from the fact that the early European explorers first thought that America was some western part of India, hence our current appellation of West Indies for the Caribbean Islands.

The Spaniards call the guinea pig *conejillo de Indias,* which means "little rabbit of India." That the Spanish thought the guinea pig looked more like a rabbit than a pig attests to the keenness of their observation.

Guinea Pigs in Medical Research

From about 1850 until World War I more and more people began to keep guinea pigs. There was ample space, particularly in rural areas, to keep them, and many a farm boy earned some extra money raising guinea pigs not only as house pets but also as laboratory animals. Guinea pigs were essential in Robert Koch's research on tuberculosis and in Louis Pasteur's research on other infectious diseases. Guinea pigs were also important to Emil von Behring in the discovery and production of a serum against diphtheria. Guinea pigs have continued to be invaluable in laboratory work ever since, and we humans owe many advances in medical science to these small, friendly animals.

Anatomy of the Guinea Pig

External Characteristics

The guinea pig is a rodent short and squat in form. Adults reach a length of 8 to 14 inches (22–35 cm). Females weigh from 1 to 2 pounds (600–1100 g), males, from 2 to 4 pounds (900–1800 g). The males usually have a larger, rounder head than the more delicate females.

The *nose* is blunt and rounded; the *mouth* is small. Like all rodents, guinea pigs have a "harelip." They also have long, prominent tactile *whiskers* at the sides of the upper lips. The *ears* are small and almost hairless. The female has only one pair of *mammary glands* and *teats* on the posterior abdominal quarter.

The *neck* is short and thus emphasizes the animal's squat shape. There is no visible *tail,* although tail vertebrae are present. The *legs* are short and relatively slender. The guinea pig walks on its *toes.* There are four toes on the front feet and three on the hind feet. The broad *toenails* have a hoof-like quality. The wild guinea pig has grey-brown *fur* with a lighter underbelly ranging from whitish to sand color. It is composed of stiff top hair and soft, silky underhair, as is the fur of the smooth-haired domestic guinea pig. The rough-coated Abyssinian guinea pig has much more outer hair; also, mutation has caused knot-like formations in the skin which are responsible in turn for the rosette patterns that cover the body of this breed. The Angora guinea pig does not shed, and its coat can grow to a length of six inches (15 cm) and more.

Internal Organs

- As a rodent the guinea pig has *gnawing* or *cutting teeth,* two each in the upper and lower jaw. These incisors are razor-sharp and are also

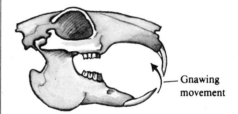

Gnawing movement

This sketch of a guinea pig skull shows the positioning of the teeth. By feeding hard foods, you help your animal keep his teeth short and sharp.

self-honing because only the front of them is covered with enamel. These teeth grow continuously, and they therefore have to be worn down by constant chewing. If the animals are not supplied with hard foods, the teeth can grow to a length that will prevent food intake. The guinea pig has no canines, but it does have eight molars both in the upper and in the lower jaw. None of the teeth have any roots.

Anatomy of the Guinea Pig

- The *ears*: Guinea pigs can hear very well. The cochlea of the guinea pig's ear has four coils in it; in humans, the cochlea has only two coils.

- The guinea pig's *lungs* have four lobes, some of which can temporarily be taken out of service by closure of the bronchial tubes. This makes the guinea pig less sensitive to some irritants, but despite this it is not good to expose guinea pigs to tobacco smoke.

- In the *stomach* the food settles in layers and remains immobile for a few hours. The complete process of digestion is quite slow and can take anywhere from five hours to seven days. Because of the more nourishing and juicier food the domestic guinea pig has been receiving for so long now, the animal has developed a larger stomach and a longer small intestine but a shorter large intestine and cecum. Therefore, the domestic guinea pig needs much less roughage than the wild cavy does.

- Many guinea pig owners find it disturbing that their pets eat their own feces. However, this is essential for the animal's health. Bacterial flora in the cecum form the important B-complex vitamins. By eating these cecal feces, which are lighter and softer than other feces, the guinea pig satisfies its need for B vitamins; and newborn guinea pigs will eat their mother's feces for the same reason.

Young
Male

Young
Female

Sexing guinea pigs: A male's testicles are visible, and the penis will emerge if you press lightly on the stomach. Also, there is a noticeable distance between the anus and the opening for the penis.

In the female, there is almost no space between the genital and anal orifices.

Anatomy of the Guinea Pig

• The guinea pig's *body temperature* normally falls between 37.8° and 40°C (100°–104°F). Guinea pigs breathe approximately 120 times per minute. This *rapid breathing* that can be observed in the movement of the nostrils is normal and not a sign of illness.

Sexing Guinea Pigs

If you are buying a guinea pig for the first time you probably will not know how to tell males from females. In adult males, the *testicles* can easily be seen on either side of the anal opening. The only sure method for sexing young males is to press gently with the thumb or thumb and forefinger just above the genital opening. This will extend the *penis* and make it visible. If the penis is retracted, the male still shows a noticeable distance between the anal and genital openings. In young males this gap is about ¼ ″ (5 mm); in older males, about ⅜ ″(10 mm).

If the animal is a female, pressure on the lower belly will reveal a slit-like genital opening that reaches almost completely to the anus (see figures on page 16).

What You Should Know and Consider Before You Buy

You will surely know before you buy a guinea pig why you want one. Perhaps you will even know what you want him to look like, what coloring and what characteristics you would like him to have. You can choose your future pet. Your guinea pig, however, does not have the luxury of choosing you. He does not know whether he will be in good hands with you or whether he can depend on you for proper care and affection over many years. He will simply have to take the owner he gets.

Some Preliminary Questions

If you have never had a pet before, you may not know if you are a reliable, patient, and sensitive pet owner. Even though a guinea pig demands only a fraction of the time, effort, and expense that a dog or cat requires, you should not underestimate or totally ignore these lesser demands. It is usually the small chores that we are most likely to neglect, so be honest with yourself as you answer these questions that will help you find out whether you will make a good guinea pig owner:

1. Are you willing to give your guinea pig constant and reliable care for the six, eight, or possibly even ten years of his life?

2. Are you aware that your guinea pig will get feebler, require more care, and become somewhat less attractive as he grows older? Will you be able to treat him with as much affection and consideration as before? An older animal will be attached to his surroundings and to you as his partner, and you should not consider getting rid of him as an option open to you, even if you know the future owners would be good to the animal.

3. Are you willing to provide the largest possible cage for your guinea pig, even though it may be quite expensive?

4. Will you allow your pet the free run of your home as often as possible, even though he may not be housebroken, may chew on furniture, and may shed on your rugs?

5. Are you willing to comb and brush your guinea pig daily? Grooming is important if your animal is going to keep a healthy, shiny coat, and it is particularly crucial for an Angora guinea pig because his long hair tends to mat easily.

6. Do you have at least one hour every day that you can devote to caring for your guinea pig, playing with him and petting him?

7. Are you willing to give up a weekend trip or even cancel a vacation if your guinea pig should get sick?

8. Would you be willing to pay for expensive veterinary treatment or surgery to save your guinea pig's life?

What You Should Know and Consider Before You Buy

9. Are you willing to care for a sick animal, even when this involves cleaning his fur soaked with urine, diarrhea discharge, and possibly pus?

10. Can you give up smoking for the sake of your guinea pig or at least avoid smoking in the room where your guinea pig is kept?

If you can honestly answer all these questions with yes, you will be a responsible pet owner and will provide a good home for a guinea pig.

A cage recommended for one or two animals. This model has a removable tray for a bottom.

Housing Your Guinea Pig

Options for Indoor Living Quarters

Guinea pig cages available in pet stores are perfectly adequate for keeping a single guinea pig. The bottom part is usually a deep tray made of hard plastic. The top is a cage of vertical bars. It clips onto the bottom and can be easily removed for cleaning. These cages are airy, easy to handle, and easy to clean. They also let the animal see out. If they are kept clean, these cages will remain odorless. A guinea pig cage should be about 2' x 1' x 1' (65 x 35 x 35 cm) and have a bottom tray about 8" (12–15 cm) deep. Do not buy smaller cages; the animal's health will suffer from lack of exercise, and the sides of the bottom tray will be so low that the guinea pig will scatter litter out of the cage every time he makes a quick movement.

When my children first wanted a guinea pig, I bought them a rectangular white plastic tub about 2½' x 1½' x 1' (70 x 50 x 23 cm). It proved to be so practical that we have raised several generations of guinea pigs in it since. The advantages of this tub are that the animal feels more secure in it than in a wire cage, litter is rarely thrown out of it, and it can be easily washed and cleaned. The disadvantages are that the guinea pig has no view of his surroundings and that it is difficult to attach a feeding dish and water container. We solved these problems by building a plywood *sleeping box* about 10" x 6" x 6" (25 x 15 x 15 cm). It had an entrance in one end and a window in the other. Whenever the animal wanted to see what was going on around him he would sit on top of his wooden house. On one of the long sides of the house we screwed on a rack for hay and greens and a bracket for a water bottle.

If you have children, you may suddenly find yourself the owner of a guinea pig your children have gotten

A small sleeping box or house with a flat roof also provides your animal with an observation platform.

as a gift from friends at school. And your children will no doubt have a ready solution to the housing problem. "There's a box in the basement that's just right for the guinea pig, and nobody is using it for anything else anyhow."

You can make do with a box for a few days, but then you should buy a suitable cage or tub. Wood is a poor material for housing guinea pigs. It is heavy and hard to clean, but worse yet it soaks up urine and soon becomes a permanent source of unpleasant odors. Even if you cover the inside of

the box with a waterproof varnish or paint, the wood will become soaked with urine sooner or later. Most paints and varnishes are not resistant to urine, and they will peel and crack. Also, the guinea pig's claws will scratch through to the untreated wood. If you still want a wooden box for your guinea pig, cover the floor with a plastic or galvanized metal tray. The advantage of a homemade wooden cage is, of course, that it can be custom-built in any size, shape, and color to fit in available space and suit individual taste. However, a urine-proof tray for the bottom should be part of your design.

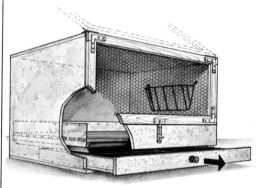

Anyone handy with tools can build this cage with its removable tray and door that can be raised on hinges.

If you decide to buy your cage, however, you will find a wide variety of guinea pig cages available at pet stores.

What You Should Know and Consider Before You Buy

A Run Outdoors

If you want to keep your guinea pig outside on your lawn during the summer months, you will need a run that is at least three feet by three feet (1 x 1 m). This can be a simple frame built of lath and covered with chicken wire. The top as well as the sides should be covered to protect your guinea pig from cats, dogs, and birds. Since a domestic guinea pig has hardly any burrowing instinct left, you do not need to anchor the bottom of the run to the ground. But do be sure that the run is on level ground. Otherwise your guinea pig can get out; and mice, rats, and weasels can get in. Because this run is moveable, you can keep shifting it around onto fresh patches of grass. If you have a large yard, you can fence in part of it as a permanent run, letting the number of guinea pigs you have and the given conditions determine the size and shape of the run. If you allow about one square yard for each animal, your lawn will not suffer appreciably. Because these larger runs are open at the top, you have to check on your animals frequently. Cats are particularly likely to get into the enclosure and bother your guinea pigs.

A Guinea Pig Hutch for Your Yard

To afford the guinea pig (or guinea pigs) in your run protection from rain, sun, wind, and predators, you can build a hutch. It should be built like a dog house, be weatherproof, and have a door about four inches (10 cm) wide and six inches (15 cm) high. You can put windows in the sides of the house or a skylight in the roof to let some light in. You should be able to flip the roof back on hinges or lift it off entirely to give you access to the hutch.

A large collapsible run for your yard with a hutch for an entire guinea pig family.

The house should have a solid floor and a sliding hatch for closing off the entrance. This hatch is particularly important if your guinea pigs will be left in the hutch at night. Also, if you have to leave your guinea pigs alone sometimes, it will put your mind at ease to know they are safe in their closed house. The hutch should be comparable to an indoor cage in size and have a floor area of at least two feet by one foot (60 x 40 cm) for a single animal.

Provide grain and drinking water for your guinea pig inside the hutch

What You Should Know and Consider Before You Buy

only. At night, you can bring your pet inside and put him in his indoor cage if you like. Do not keep you pet outside, either in his run or in his hutch, during the winter months. The optimum temperature for guinea pigs is about 68°F (18°–20°C). They will fare very well in temperatures down to 50°F (10°C), but they should not be exposed to anything below that.

Other Supplies You Will Need

Containers for Food and Water

Try to have all your supplies on hand before you bring your pet home. All too often, owners of guinea pigs start out with makeshift supplies and then never bother to get proper equipment. That makes life harder both for you and your animals. Instead of buying the solid earthenware *bowls* specially designed for rabbits and guinea pigs, some guinea pig owners will make do with plastic or glass bowls that are too light and not stable enough. As a result, the animal often winds up pawing through his litter for his food. If these same bowls are used as water containers, they will often be tipped over, or the water will become contaminated with litter or feces. *Water bottles* made of glass or plastic are much better. They are equipped with bent sipper tubes of glass or metal from which the guinea pig takes

Heavy glass or earthenware bowls with wide bottoms are recommended for feeding. Normal bowls tip easily and are unsuitable.

Provide water in water bottles with sipper tubes. In bowls, it soon becomes contaminated. Various types of water bottles available in pet stores are shown.

water one drop at a time. These water bottles come in a variety of sizes and can be attached to cage bars or to a wall with clamps. Greens should be fed in a *rack,* which is often included with a cage, but pet stores also sell these racks separately. Do not just scatter greens on the bottom of the cage; they will get dirty and make your pet ill. Fermenting greens are a frequent cause of intestinal disorders.

Accessories for Grooming and General Care

Many owners of guinea pigs complain that their pets shed a great deal, but it never occurs to these people to brush or comb their pets regularly. If you give your guinea pig the daily treat of grooming his fur, you will

Tools for daily grooming. Regular combing and brushing is especially important for Angora guinea pigs.

soon see how shiny and healthy his coat can look. Use a *medium-hard brush* for smooth-haired guinea pigs (as you would for small dog breeds). Rosette-haired guinea pigs have to be brushed lightly but also need combing. Long-haired Angora guinea pigs should be combed only with a *long-toothed comb.*

To clean the cage you will need a *brush,* a *scraper,* and a *disinfectant.* It is surprising how quickly even a plastic tub will get dirty without the appropriate cleaning. Urinary deposits collect in the corners of the cage or tub, and soon a strong odor pervades the room. You can avoid this by thorough and regular cleaning.

Male or Female?

You should decide before you buy your animal whether you prefer a male or a female. *Females* have certain advantages for keeping indoors. They remain smaller; they do not smell as strong as the males when they reach sexual maturity; and they are usually more affectionate. There is always the danger, of course, that your children may come home from a friend's house with a pregnant female. All it takes is one playmate who happens to own a male guinea pig.

Males are larger and develop a stronger odor as they mature, but they also tend to be livelier. If you want to eliminate the odor, have your male castrated at the age of nine to twelve months.

Will Two Guinea Pigs Be Happier Than One?

A *single guinea pig* is the best choice if you want a pet and playmate for your child or if you plan to spend a lot of time with your guinea pig and want it to develop a strong attachment to you. The single animal will come to see you as his partner and primary attachment and will become an affectionate pet. However, if your guinea pig will be along much of the time because you are away at work or because your children are in school or busy with homework, you should consider getting a second animal. Guinea pigs are gregarious creatures that live in clans in the wild. They usually get along well and enjoy a lot of contact with each other, and you can count on two guinea pigs being happier together than if they lived alone.

If you decide to keep two animals, the most likely combinations are *two females, two neutered males,* or *a female and a neutered male.* If you have a female and an uncastrated male, you can expect four or five litters of young each year. Observing the birth process and the family life of guinea pigs can be a happy and memorable experience for you and especially for your children. But certain conditions have to be met. You have to have enough space and plenty of time, and you will have to find homes for the young when they mature.

I would advise against keeping *two males* because they start fighting as soon as they begin to mature. And these fights are often ferocious battles with tooth and claw and are by no means harmless. You will then have no choice but to give away one of the animals or to have them both neutered.

Short Hair, Rosettes, or Long Hair?

It is a matter of taste whether you decide to get a short-haired guinea pig or one with a rosette-patterned coat. There is no difference in the care required. A *short-haired guinea pig* looks comparatively slim, and its fur is easy to take care of, as is the coat of the rosette or Abyssinian guinea pig. Due to mutation, its fur grows in rosettes that can occur on all parts of the body. Because of these whorls, the Abyssinian guinea pig is a rather droll and shaggy little creature and looks a

Guinea pigs are happier kept in pairs. A pair is shown here in typical sleeping position.

What You Should Know and Consider Before You Buy

little chubbier than a smooth-haired animal.

Angora guinea pigs have soft, silky hair that grows up to six inches (15 cm) in length. They need constant grooming to preserve the beauty of their coats. Wood shavings and straw make better litter for these animals than do sawdust or peat because they can be more easily combed out of the long hair. Angora guinea pigs can also be kept on a hardwood grating that lets urine and feces fall into peat or another type of litter kept in a tray below. The hardwood grating has to be treated with a protective water-proof coating and washed every day. (For more information on guinea pig breeds, see pages 58–59.)

Age and Time of Purchase

Buy a young animal whenever possible. At about two to four months, the animal is still considerably smaller than a fully grown one and weighs between 11 and 22 ounces (300–600 g). A guinea pig is full grown at eight months. An adult female will weigh about 28 ounces (800 g); a male, about 2 pounds (1000 g). As they get older, they get heavier. Some males can weigh as much as 4 pounds (1800 g).

A Checklist for When You Buy

• Whether you buy a young animal or an older one, it must be healthy.

• Be sure that the animal has clear eyes with no signs of sticky discharge around them.

• Nose, lips, and ears should be free of inflammation and incrustations.

• The coat should be shiny and clean. Marked shedding, thin fur, and bald spots are signs of illness or old age.

• It is particularly important that the anal area be clean and dry. Diarrhea is a serious illness in guinea pigs.

• Check the animal's toes and claws. Older animals often have calloused toes that are in abnormal positions. This is a result of the claws having been allowed to grow too long in the past.

• Check to see if the animal is still a quick and agile runner. Some guinea pigs soon breathe heavily after running a little. This may be due to illness or obesity.

Adjusting to the New Home

Young animals of various colorations: ▷
Above: A Red Abyssinian and a black, smooth-haired animal.
Below: A tricolored English Check (or Tortoiseshell-and-White) and a Silver Agouti.

First Days at Home

A guinea pig will be somewhat frightened when you first take him from the carrier in which you brought him home and put him in his new cage, tub, or hutch. Leave him alone at first. He needs some undisturbed time to get used to his new surroundings. This may take only a few hours, or, in some cases, it may take several days. At any rate, the animal will be grateful if you provide him with a lot of straw or hay into which he can crawl and hide at first. Feeling safe there, he can begin to take in his new environment. If you plan to provide your animal with a sleeping box, wait until he will come to your hand, that is, until he is completely at ease with you and in his environment. If you give him his little box when you bring him home or too soon after that, the animal will remain shy and stay in his hiding place much of the time.

He can still his first pangs of hunger with hay, too; and he will nibble on the hay in the process of making a "bed" for himself. This nibbling will occupy and relax him, thus helping him get used to his new home. Watch your new companion closely during this time. If he emerges from his layer of hay or straw and expresses curiosity about his wider environment, carefully take him out of his cage, put him down next to it, and let him move around in the room you will keep him in. Like a wild guinea pig in his natural habitat, your pet will take only a few cautious exploratory steps and always with some kind of cover, as along a wall. Then he will return to his cage, the scent of which is now familiar to him. He will run in the same direction once again or perhaps several times more, advancing a few steps each time, but then he will always quickly return to his cage.

This is the right way to pick up a guinea pig. It is important to enclose the entire body with your hand.

Next, he will move in the opposite direction, again under cover of the wall or some furniture. This is how a guinea pig establishes his "paths" and explores his new surroundings. It may take some time, perhaps several days,

26

before he is ready to run across the open floor of the room.

What I have said here applies to guinea pigs that are about four to six weeks old, are still acting on their instincts, and have yet to form a close bond with a human being. Some animals, of course, are already fully familiar with humans and will feel at home immediately in a new environment.

And just the opposite is possible, too. Some guinea pigs are so terrified and timid that they almost die of fright and do not dare to come out of the corner of their cage. These animals should, of course, be left alone and not be taken out of their cages immediately. You will have to be careful and, sometimes, infinitely patient in

Guinea pigs like to stretch a lot, especially after they have been sleeping in a squatting position.

helping them adapt to their environment. Observe your animal carefully. He will usually let you know when he has overcome his shyness by coming out of hiding and starting to look around (see also "Understanding Guinea Pigs," page 60).

Winning Your Guinea Pig's Trust

After your guinea pig has spent some time in his cage, you can approach him slowly and talk to him in a calm, quiet tone. Cautiously offer him a treat: a carrot, a piece of apple, a bit of lettuce. The animal will be attracted by the sight and smell of the food, will overcome his fear of this strange hand, and will take the treat. If your guinea pig is hesitant, leave the food in front of him and pull your hand back a little. Watch your new companion's reaction and — most important of all — be patient. With time, even the most timid of guinea pigs will eventually take food from your hand. When he does, you will know you have won his trust and confidence. He will let you pet him, and he may even nudge his head or flank against your hand, let you pick him up on your arm, or hold him on your lap.

With some few guinea pigs none of these tactics will be successful, and you will have to resort to friendly but forceful persuasion. Take the animal

Adjusting to the New Home

onto your lap; pet him; and talk to him in a calm, soothing way. This approach is almost always successful with timid guinea pigs. The animal learns that he has nothing to fear from humans. Some animals need only two or three such "treatments" before they become tame. Others may need much more attention. These animals come to trust people only very slowly, so do not try to hurry things along. Be patient, and take your time.

How to Pick Up and Carry a Guinea Pig

If you want to pick up your guinea pig, put one hand around his chest, lift him up, and support his hindquarters with your other hand. His hind feet should be in the palm of your hand (see color photograph, page 9).

If you want to carry your guinea pig for any distance, put him on your

This is the way adults should carry a guinea pig. Children should use both hands.

forearm, and use your other hand to hold him from above. Children can carry the animal more securely if it can place all four feet against their chests and be supported with both hands. Better still, use a basket. With a basket, a child can carry a guinea pig around for quite some time without any danger to the animal. Guinea pigs are not as agile and as adept at jumping as cats, and they can be seriously injured by a fall. Broken bones, paralysis, or even death can be the result.

Guinea Pigs and Other Pets

Other pets that you can easily keep along with a guinea pig are *ornamental fish, amphibians and reptiles* in terrariums, and small *birds. Golden hamsters* and *deer mice,* however, are not good company for our friendly rodent. Deer mice are particularly prone to attacking him, and he will not defend himself against them because his behavioral patterns do not match those of deer mice. Life with a *dwarf rabbit* will usually be harmonious and peaceful, but occasionally a rabbit will bite a guinea pig. We once had a rabbit that attacked our guinea pig ferociously every time we turned them out to run together. And despite our most patient efforts, we could not induce our rabbit to have any friendly feelings for our guinea pig. The rabbit at-

Adjusting to the New Home

tacked other guinea pigs, too; and this led us to believe that he did not just have a "personal aversion" for our guinea pig but harbored a dislike for the species as such.

A guinea pig may get along well with a *dog* or a *cat,* just as he may with a rabbit. But then again peaceful coexistence may be out of the question. Whether such an arrangement will work or not will depend entirely on the individual animals involved. The guinea pig will hardly ever be the one to break the peace. If a dog and a guinea pig grow up together, you will have no problems. But if you bring a guinea pig into a home where a dog has lived for a long time, the dog's training and character will determine how he will get along with his new housemate. There will be few problems if the dog has been well trained and understands immediately that he cannot harm the new pet. It is important that you not ignore your dog or favor the guinea pig by petting it a lot in the dog's presence. Your dog should continue to receive the same attention and affection he is accustomed to. The guinea pig will have to stay in his cage at first, and you may even want to put the cage in a room where the dog is not allowed. If your dog is small, your guinea pig's cage will be safe on a table. You will have to be present when the animals are brought together so that you can in-tervene instantly if things go wrong. Dogs and guinea pigs will often develop a friendly relationship. The guinea pig loses his fear completely, and the dog assumes the role of protector.

Cats are usually quite indifferent to guinea pigs, but guinea pigs can sometimes make friends with them, too. I was once witness to an extremely close friendship between a cat and a guinea pig. The two animals would lie snuggled up to each other, the cat licking the guinea pig and allowing him to nurse. The cat had clearly "adopted" the guinea pig and treated it as if it had been her own kitten. Since cats are highly individualistic, there is very little we can do to influence their relationship to guinea pigs one way or the other.

A *parrot* or *macaw* can be a real danger to a guinea pig newly introduced into your home. Jealousy may prompt the bird to attack the guinea pig and injure it severely with its beak. In cases like this it is essential that the owner be particularly affectionate and patient with the bird. If the bird is the newcomer, essentially the same principles apply. A lot of affection for both animals, a great deal of patience, and constant attention on your part will help avoid potentially dangerous situations. Obviously, your bird and guinea pig should never be left together unattended.

Adjusting to the New Home

Dangers in Your Home

I have emphasized in the previous sections of this chapter that you should always watch your guinea pig whenever he is out of his cage. Be sure to keep an eye on him whenever he has the run of your home, for it happens all too often that we or our children or a guest *steps on* a guinea pig in a moment of inattentiveness. Occasionally, too, the animal will get *caught in a door.* Being affectionate animals, guinea pigs will follow us around, and if we happen to forget about them, the accidents just described are likely to occur. Be sure to tell your visitors that your guinea pig is running around loose in your house or yard. You will spare your pet pain and your guests and yourself unhappy experiences.

Guinea pigs love to *gnaw* on things. This can be dangerous for them if they happen to *gnaw on an electric cord.* I have never lost a guinea pig due to an electric shock, but our first few pet guinea pigs did chew some cords down to the bare wire before I realized what was going on. I learned my lesson, and I have never left extension cords or other wires lying on my floors since. They are either raised off the floor now or hidden behind baseboards. Do not let your animals run

The danger of injuring an animal by stepping on him is great because tame guinea pigs like to follow people around and cannot be relied on to stay out of harm's way.

Be careful shutting doors. Guinea pigs are unaware of this danger and can easily be caught and crushed.

32

Adjusting to the New Home

loose if you are vacuuming or using any other appliances that leave wires exposed on the floor. Then, too, electric wiring that has been gnawed at is dangerous for us. It can cause shorts and even start fires in our homes.

Guinea pigs also like to nibble on paper of any kind. They are particularly fond of wallpaper. They quickly learn how to locate the bottom edge of it and can then skillfully tear off whole strips of wallpaper. *Eating wallpaper* is not harmful to them, but it is hard on our living quarters. Guinea pigs also enjoy chewing on furniture, especially upholstered pieces. I once had a guinea pig who took a liking to a particular *rug*. Before long the rug was a tattered rag.

Books we were careless enough to leave on the floor interested our guinea pigs, too; and many a missing or chewed-on page remains to us as a lasting monument to one of our guinea pigs.

Guinea pigs can also cause more or less severe damage if they are *not housebroken*. Their longish *feces* are dry, almost odorless, and leave relatively few traces behind. Their *urine* is a different matter. Its corrosive quality and strong odor can ruin carpeting, and even synthetic flooring and wood flooring can be permanently damaged by the stains it leaves.

Death by electric shock. A guinea pig cannot be expected to know the difference between an electrical wire and a harmless twig.

Proper Nutrition

Guinea pigs are not fussy eaters, and they are also vegetarians. They can live entirely on fresh and dried plants, just as their wild relatives do. If you feed your guinea pig *fresh greens, dry food,* and *grains* regularly, you can feel sure that your pet is getting an ample and well-balanced diet (see the Food Chart on page 38). You can find a variety of good commercial feeds in your pet store.

Fresh Food

Fresh foods include *grasses, herbs, fruits, green vegetables, root vegetables,* and *potatoes.* In the summer, greens such as *grass, clover, dandelion greens, nettles,* and many *herbs* can make up the main part of your guinea pig's diet. Many greens can be picked in meadows and along country roads, but never pick greens along heavily traveled roads or highways where the plants may be poisoned by automobile exhausts. Also do not pick greens in areas frequented by dogs. Dog feces and urine contain many harmful bacteria and parasites. Remember, too, that herbicides and insecticides are dangerous for your guinea pig and that, when sprayed, they can be carried a long way on the wind. Even products from your own garden may not be safe if traces of in-secticide from your neighbor's yard have reached them.

If you cannot pick greens from a garden or meadow, you can feed your guinea pig store-bought greens: *lettuce, endive, chicory, carrots, potatoes, vegetable peelings, apples, pears, turnips, beets, cucumbers,* and so on. Even in the winter, there is plenty of produce to choose from. Introduce clover and the different kinds of cabbage into the diet very gradually to avoid bloating.

Dry Feeds

Good hay made up of varied grasses will be the mainstay of your animal's diet all year long. Even if he has an abundance of fresh greens, he will always enjoy some hay, which acts as a balance to the juicy greens. In the winter, your guinea pig can fare very well on water and hay. So, as you can see, hay is your guinea pig's "daily bread." Guinea pigs like clover hay as well as grass hay, and dry bean and pea vines are welcome changes in their menu, too. The hay you use cannot be musty, moldy, or dust laden. Be sure to store it in a dry, well-ventilated place. Good hay has an aromatic smell to it. *Moldy hay* can be fatal, and many guinea pigs die every year from having eaten moldy hay.

Proper Nutrition

High-Protein Foods

Wheat, corn, oats, peanuts, soy beans, sunflower seeds, pellets made up of one or more grains, potato flakes, and *dry breads* are all high-protein foods. The simplest way to provide protein is in pellet feeds available in pet stores. Only if you have a large number of guinea pigs is it economical to buy mixed feed in 50- or 100-pound (25 or 50 kg) bags or to buy different grains in large quantities and then mix them yourself to suit the needs of your animals.

Dry pellets, depending on the mixture in them, can provide either all or almost all of the vitamins, minerals, and trace elements your animals need. If you breed large numbers of guinea pigs, you should choose an all-in-one pellet that will provide a balanced and sufficiently nutritious diet. This kind of feed requires the least amount of work and is the most economical.

For you as a pet owner, feeding is one of the most important means of contact you have with your guinea pig. If you offer your pet different foods, you will quickly learn what he likes best. By hand-feeding your guinea pig you will create a special bond that cannot be developed between you and your pet in any other way. For both you and your pet, feeding times should be the high points of your daily interaction.

What to Feed and How Much

Guinea pigs are undemanding not only in the type of food they require but also in the amount. Here are some guidelines:

• Feed as much in the way of greens and hay as your pet will eat. Do not, however, just throw greens on the cage floor where they will be contaminated with feces and urine. Also, damp greens rot very quickly if an animal lies on them and warms them. A rack placed on the side of the cage will keep greens and/or hay clean yet readily accessible. Hay is not as quick to rot as greens and can be spread lightly on the floor over the litter, but as food it should be put in a feeding rack.

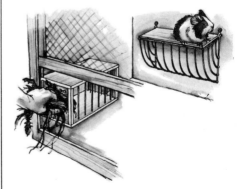

Two practical feeding racks for guinea pigs. The cover keeps the animals from contaminating their greens.

35

Proper Nutrition

• A guinea pig should get about two ounces (40–70 g; one to two handfuls) of vegetable parings and other fresh foods daily. Amounts will vary depending on the size of your animal and the nutritional value of the food offered (see Food Chart, page 38).

• High-protein food is essential, but only very small amounts are required. One or two tablespoonfuls of pellets, mixed grains, or dry bread are sufficient. Do not give in to your pet's pathetic, squeaking demands for more. If you give him too much high-calorie food, especially oats, sunflower seeds, or peanuts, your guinea pig will soon be overweight and, consequently, more susceptible to illness. Some pet owners share sweets, bread and butter, and cold cuts with their guinea pigs. While this may not be an immediate cause of disease, the resulting obesity will make the animal more susceptible to disease. Also, the feces will have an abnormally strong odor.

• Some animal protein can be quite beneficial. Pellet feeds usually contain five percent animal protein. If you feed a grain mixture, you should give your guinea pig an occasional dog biscuit to meet this animal protein requirement. This addition to the diet will give your animals beautifully luxuriant fur. Young and growing guinea pigs also require small amounts of animal protein.

What and How Much Should a Guinea Pig Drink?

Guinea pigs do not drink much at all, and if they have enough grass and greens to eat they can get along fine without any additional water. You should, however, make *water* available to them at all times. Although a heavy, broad-based bowl can be used for water, it is not altogether practical because the water is soon dirtied with litter and feces and has to be changed often. A suspended water bottle with a curved sipper tube is preferable. Your pet will quickly learn to drink from these bottles. The high chlorine content of much tap water is harmful to your pet and should be reduced by letting the water stand for a while, or you can boil it and let it cool before you fill the bottle with it. Instead of water, you can give your guinea pig *milk,* which provides both animal protein and fluid for your pet. Whole

Guinea pigs drink by licking drops of water from the sipper tube of the water bottle.

36

Proper Nutrition

milk is not suitable because of its high fat content. Either dilute regular milk with two parts water to one part milk, or buy pasteurized skim milk. Do not let the milk go sour because sour milk causes diarrhea.

Although some guinea pigs drink hardly anything, others develop such a taste for liquids that they immediately drink up whatever is put before them. Cut those "heavy drinkers" back to small rations of liquids, and stand firm no matter how pitifully they squeak.

Friends of ours used to give their guinea pig a beer glass to lick out. It got so fond of beer that it begged for more whenever there was beer on the table. Once it got the glass, it licked it out so thoroughly that not a trace of beer was left. The result of this "cute" performance was that the man of the house indulged the animal by drinking more beer, and the animal died prematurely of a liver ailment.

This example shows how easy it is to harm an animal either through thoughtlessness or misguided affection. *We cannot rely on an animal instinctively refusing things that are bad for it.* The animal's health is in the hands of the owner, and there is no more important prerequisite for an animal's health than a sensible diet designed for the particular species.

Feeding Guide

• Always feed at fixed times.
• Feeding twice a day is advisable, especially during warm weather when fresh foods spoil quickly.
• Remove leftover perishable foods every day.
• Give fresh water every day.
• Occasionally put twigs from poplars, willows, or fruit trees in the cage. These provide minerals, and gnawing on them helps the animal keep its teeth in good shape.
• Some guinea pigs will touch a salt-lick only rarely or not at all, but most of them will use it a great deal, and one should always be available.

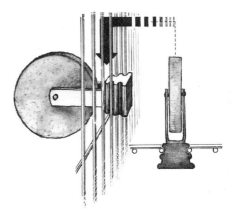

Salt licks help avoid deficiencies in minerals and trace elements. You can attach one to the cage bars with a clamp.

Proper Nutrition

Food Chart

Food Type	% Protein	% Carbohydrates	Daily Requirement in ounces (in grams)
High-Protein Foods			
Wheat	10	73	½–¾ (10–20)
Oats	9	54	¼–½ (8–15)
Barley	7	68	½–1 (12–25)
Corn	9	65	½–¾ (10–20)
Peanuts	20	15	¼ (5)
Sunflower seeds	16	21	¼ (5)
Potato flakes	3	48	½–1 (12–25)
Dry whole wheat bread	8	55	½–¾ (10–20)
Pellets	20	48	1–2 (20–40)
Dry Foods			
Meadow hay	5	31	¾–2 (20–50)
Clover hay	9	37	¾–1½ (20–40)
Nettles hay	17	33	½–1¼ (10–30)
Alfalfa hay	4	10	¾–2 (20–50)
Dry bean vines	4	15	¾–2 (20–50)
Wheat straw	0.5	13	unlimited
Oats straw	1	18	unlimited
Fresh Foods (Greens, Vegetables, Fruits)			
Grass	2	8	2–3 (50–80)
Clover	3	10	1½–2¾ (40–70)
Dandelion greens	4	10	1–2 (30–60)
Coltsfoot	2	8	2–3 (50–80)
Plantain	2	8	2–3 (50–80)
Nettles	4	8	1–2 (30–60)
Lettuce	2	8	2–3 (50–80)
Carrots	1	8	2–3 (50–80)
Turnips	0.7	9	2–3 (50–80)
Potatoes (boiled)	1.6	21	1–1½ (20–40)
Potatoes (raw)	1.2	15	1–1½ (20–50)
Apples	0.2	12	1½–2½ (40–70)
Pears	0.5	14	1–2 (30–60)

Diseases of the Guinea Pig

Health through Exercise and Good Nutrition

Guinea pigs are rarely sick. While there are many diseases that can befall these small rodents, they can easily be prevented by adequate housing and care. With guinea pigs, as with all pets, an attentive and observant owner is the animal's best protection against disease. If you handle your animal daily, you will immediately notice any changes in behavior or external appearance. You can often help your animal with a simple home remedy or by simply recognizing and removing the cause of the problem. If, however, you cannot determine the cause of an illness, you should consult a veterinarian.

The most common causes of illness in guinea pigs are *lack of exercise* and/or *incorrect nutrition.* Guinea pigs are agile creatures and take pleasure in physical activity. But if they are constantly confined in too small a cage, they will get fat, lazy, and stiff. This condition can be the beginning of a slow decline that ends in premature death. Since nuts and grains are easy to feed and people worry too much that their animal is going hungry, a guinea pig often gets as much food as it demands and soon turns into a fat, lethargic animal. Pet owners themselves have often informed me that they give their guinea pigs chocolates, other candies, beer, and even hard liquor "because the animals like these things so much." One wonders how the poor creatures developed these tastes in the first place.

Deficiency Diseases

Paradoxical as it may seem, it is usually the obese, overfed guinea pigs that suffer from deficiency diseases. The reason for this is that they have been fed an *imbalanced diet* high in calories but low in the greens and fruits that supply vitamins. *Insufficient quantities of minerals and trace elements* can result in ill health. A balanced diet that includes fresh foods will prevent deficiency diseases.

• *Vitamin A deficiency* produces lethargy, cramps, paralysis, and shortness of breath. Vitamin A is beneficial to the epithelia and affects the functions of the skin and mucous membranes. Vitamin A is present as a provitamin in greens, especially in lettuce, endive, and carrots.

• *Vitamin B complex deficiencies* can cause hair loss, skin problems, diarrhea and other intestinal disorders, weight loss, growth problems, anemia, cramps, and paralysis. The various vitamins of the B-complex complement each other. All of the necessary B-complex vitamins are contained in food yeast, wheat germ, bran, grains, milk, and greens.

• The guinea pig is the only rodent that cannot produce its own vitamin C and therefore has to take in sufficient quantities of vitamin C in foods like greens, cabbage, carrots, and potatoes. Winter is the season when guinea pigs are most likely to suffer from *vitamin C deficiency,* which can in turn lead to illness and death. The most common consequences of this deficiency are scurvy, reduced resistance to infectious diseases, colds, internal bleeding, and bleeding gums. A sign of vitamin C deficiency is lying a lot on one side and stretching out the legs.

• *Vitamin D deficiency* and the rickets it induces rarely occur in guinea pigs because there are adequate amounts of calcium and phosphorus in the grains, hay, and greens the animal usually eats. Much more common are the complications that result when supplementary vitamin D is added to the food (e.g., in cod liver oil). The phosphorus level becomes too high, and the bones lose their calcium.

• Possible consequences of *vitamin E deficiency* are stunted growth, infertility, fetal death in the womb, poor equilibrium, and paralysis. Fresh wheat germ is rich in vitamin E and should therefore be part of your guinea pig's diet. Other grains also contain vitamin E, though in lesser quantities.

• *Vitamin K deficiency* can easily be prevented by feeding fresh greens. Guinea pigs that are fed nothing but hay and old grains can, however, develop nose bleeds and digestive problems.

Internal Diseases

Internal diseases are difficult to diagnose, and if you detect *diarrhea, shortness of breath, fever,* or *paralysis,* you should take the animal to a veterinarian immediately. Do not try to treat these symptoms with home remedies. You are liable to prolong the illness and lessen the chances for recovery. These symptoms usually indicate *infections* caused by viruses, bacteria, or parasites. Illnesses of this kind demand prompt and exact diagnosis and treatment with appropriate medication. Antibiotics, sulfonamides, furazolidine, and other such medications should be administered in strict accordance with your veterinarian's instructions.

Diarrhea

Diarrhea is usually caused by *bacterial* or *parasitic infections of the intestines.* If your guinea pig has eaten spoiled or improper food, thin black

Diseases of the Guinea Pig

tea, zwieback, grated apples, and hay may help. The stool should, however, be examined by a veterinarian so that correct medication can be administered if infection is present.

Colds

Guinea pigs do, unfortunately, contract colds quite often. These colds are usually caused by *viral or bacterial infections* and have to be treated as serious illnesses. If your guinea pig becomes lethargic, has a ruffled coat, starts to sneeze and cough, has a runny nose and possibly enteritis and diarrhea, take him to your veterinarian immediately. Home remedies such as camomile tea, an infrared heat lamp, and a piece of bread soaked with cough syrup will not cure the disease, but they can help diminish the discomfort. What is essential here is an antibiotic in the form of an injection or a prescription drug. Without prompt treatment of this kind guinea pigs will often die of colds. Colds result from exposure to low temperatures, drafts, damp weather, and dampness underfoot (e.g., excessively wet grass in an outdoor run). Guinea pigs should not be bathed. They can swim if they have to, but they do not like the water, and baths are a frequent cause of colds.

Viral Paralysis

While some kind of rodent virus that induces paralysis occurs fairly often in guinea pigs, a polio-like paralysis does not. If your pet shows any signs of paralysis, consult your veterinarian for a diagnosis.

If your guinea pig shows the slightest signs of paralysis, take him to a veterinarian immediately.

Intestinal Parasites

Tapeworms, roundworms, and pinworms are found only rarely in guinea pigs, and these parasites are not transmissible to humans. If you find worms in your pet's stool or litter, take the animal to your veterinarian.

Severe parasitic infestation can produce diarrhea, anemia, and weight loss. Animals that are outdoors a lot are more frequently affected than are animals that are kept indoors.

Important Tips for General Care

Disorders of an external nature can often be treated at home. However, if you are uncertain about the exact

Diseases of the Guinea Pig

nature or treatment of the disorder, consult your veterinarian.

Broken Teeth

A guinea pig will break an incisor tooth only rarely. If this should happen, you need not worry because it will grow back, just as any of the other teeth do. However, you have to watch that the opposing tooth does not grow too long in the meantime. If it does, you must clip it back to the correct length as described below in the section "Overgrown Teeth." *A broken tooth does not call for a change to soft foods,* as is often assumed. Such a change would permit all the other teeth to grow too long, and then they would have to be clipped, too. If your guinea pig breaks teeth frequently, he needs additional minerals and trace elements. Try giving him mineral water (uncarbonated) instead of tap water. You can also get appropriate food supplements from your pet store. If teeth continue to break despite adequate mineral intake, consult your veterinarian.

Overgrown Teeth

Your guinea pig's teeth will grow too long only if you fail to give him enough hard foods and things to gnaw on. If he always gets *grain, twigs, wood,* and *hard bread crusts,* the teeth will get the natural wear they need and will remain sharp and the right length.

But if you feed only milk-soaked bread, greens, fruit, vegetables, and hay, the teeth will suffer. I have seen guinea pigs grind their teeth together in an effort to keep them worn down properly, but this attempt at self-help does not do the job. The teeth grow longer until the animal can no longer gnaw or even close its mouth. The only solution at this point is to clip the teeth before the animal starves. This is easily done with sharp clippers, but it takes some practice, and you should learn how to do it from an experienced guinea pig breeder, an attendant in your pet store, or a veterinarian. Some guinea pigs have unusually short lower jaws, and their teeth will grow too long even if they are given hard foods and twigs to gnaw on. With such animals, the teeth will have to be clipped every two to three months.

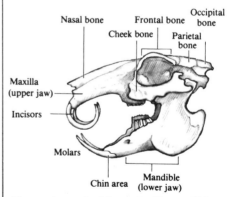

Abnormal growth of the teeth will occur if they are not worn down by constant gnawing.

42

Diseases of the Guinea Pig

Overgrown Nails

The toenails often grow too long, causing the guinea pig to walk on the sides of his feet and with much discomfort. Unless this condition is corrected, serious deformities and inflammations can occur. It is quite easy to spare your animal these pains.

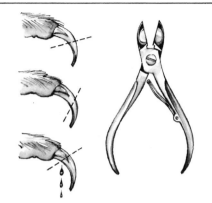

This is how you should hold your animal when you trim his nails.

Cut his *nails regularly,* and his feet will stay healthy. Use sharp nail clippers because the nails are very tough. Do not cut them off too short, or you may cut into blood vessels or nerve endings. If you hold light-colored nails up to the light, you can easily see the quick. With dark toenails, it is safer to clip them more frequently and not cut them back too short. If you should cut a nail too short and it bleeds, you can hold a cotton swab soaked in iron chloride or peroxide against it for a couple of minutes.

Above: Correct trimming with nail clippers. Incorrect trimming (middle) can splinter the nail or (below) injure the blood vessels.

Ectoparasites

Guinea pigs can become infested with fleas, mites, ticks, and lice. *Lice* and *fleas* occur very rarely if you keep your animal clean, but guinea pigs can occasionally suffer a massive infestation of cat fleas. Animals with either lice or fleas will be restless, will scratch a lot, bite their fur, and shake themselves. Heavy infestations can have serious consequences. The parasites suck the blood, thus weakening the animal and making it susceptible to infections the insects are carrying.

Fur and Skin Mites

Various *mites* can infest guinea pigs, depending on the genetic background of your guinea pig strain, on the general health of your animal, and on the number and type of other

Diseases of the Guinea Pig

animal species your guinea pig comes in contact with. Hair loss and skin irritations are typical signs of mite infestation. Crusts or scabs may form on the back of the nose, around the mouth, or only around ears or down the back. The lesion will be most visible where the guinea pig can scratch at it. These parasites can be combatted with various modern *insecticides* in liquid or powder form. You must follow the instructions carefully to prevent freshly laid insect eggs from hatching.

Guinea pigs that are kept outdoors can become infested with *ticks,* especially if you live near wooded areas. Examine your animal carefully to check for such parasites.

If your guinea pigs live indoors, you can prevent parasite infestations by using *insecticide strips* in the house and will never have to resort to

For daily grooming, hold the guinea pig on your hand and arm, and do not brush too vigorously.

powders or liquids on the animals. These strips usually prevent insect infestations, too, on all other pets and on people as well. Remember, though, that there must be adequate ventilation. A cellar or attic room where there is no air exchange is not a suitable place for an insecticide strip.

If you find that mites have gotten into your animal's ears and there are already scabs or discharges in the ear, then you should take the animal to the veterinarian to get the ears cleaned and treated. If you try to do this yourself, you can damage the interior of the ear irreversibly.

Minor Wounds

Minor accidents or biting among animals may leave small cuts that usually heal quickly by themselves. *Cotton soaked with peroxide* can be used to help stop persistent bleeding. If a wound does not heal easily and gives off a bloody or pussy discharge, then you should consult a veterinarian who will clean the lesion and prescribe an appropriate topical ointment. Ointments you might use yourself can be effective, too.

Fungal Skin Lesions

Guinea pigs can be affected by the same fungal infections that humans get. Sometimes these lesions cannot be distinguished from those caused by mites. Do not wait too long before

Diseases of the Guinea Pig

Bald spots can be caused by skin fungi, skin mites, and hair mites.

you consult a veterinarian, for delayed diagnosis and treatment reduce the chances of a cure. Prescription drugs are needed to treat these lesions.

Taking Your Guinea Pig to the Veterinarian

If you have to take your guinea pig to the veterinarian, put him in a basket with a lid on it or, better yet, into a carrier that you can buy in a pet store. Guinea pigs can become very frightened in a strange environment and especially so in a waiting room full of dogs and cats. They may well try to jump out of a container, so do not open the container until you are in the examining room. Under no circumstances should you carry your guinea pig to the veterinarian's office in your arms, nor should you remove him from his container to show to

people in the waiting room. Do not assume either that your animal will feel safer on your lap. This mistaken idea could well add a fall — and hence a contusion or bone fracture — to your animal's troubles.

It is very important to follow closely any instructions your veterinarian gives you for the treatment of your sick animal and the administration of medications. The veterinarian will do everything in his power to help your animal, but you have to be patient because a rapid cure is often not possible. Sometimes it takes a lot of time even to find the cause of a problem.

If your guinea pig is suffering a great deal and the veterinarian sees little chance of improvement, it is better to let the animal be put to sleep rather than prolong its suffering.

Vacation Care for Your Guinea Pig

Traveling with a Guinea Pig

Guinea pigs bear up quite well under travel and the climactic changes often involved with it. You need have no qualms about taking your pet with you on vacation and keeping him in his cage in your hotel room. There are guinea pig cages available that fold up into the bottom pan, and they can even be carried in a suitcase. Other guests will not be bothered by your animal. Cat and dog owners do not have such an easy lot. Most hotels and motels will not permit cats or dogs on the premises because other guests may object to them. You should, of course, still ask your host or hotel manager if it is all right for you to bring your guinea pig.

If you are planning to *travel to a foreign country* with your guinea pig,

A practical carrier for a visit to your veterinarian or for short trips.

you should inquire at the appropriate consulate and find out what papers you will need (certificate of health, etc.) so that you can cross the border and return home again with your animal.

Travel by Car, Train, or Airplane

If you have decided to take your guinea pig along on a trip, you will also have to take whatever supplies you need as well as your animal's usual grain and hay. Greens and fruit you can buy wherever you go. If you *travel by train,* you should either buy or build a carrier. In either case it should have air holes or a panel of wire mesh at the top for ventilation. The bottom should be covered with a thick layer of litter plus a little hay on top of that. For food, take some grain and carrots and/or apples. Water should not be necessary.

If you *travel by car,* you can leave the guinea pig in the cage it uses at home. Just set the cage inside a carton open on top, and put the whole package on the back seat. This way, someone in the back seat can attend to the animal and keep it company on the trip. Or, if you prefer, you can use a carrier for car trips, too.

You may not be able to take your guinea pig along if you *travel by air.* Every airline has its particular rules and regulations. Some airlines will allow you to take your pet into the passengers' cabin in an appropriate carrier. Others transport animals only in the luggage compartment or in special compartments that cost extra. These differences in policy make it essential that you check with the airline when you are planning your trip.

Alternative Care

Relatives and Friends

If you cannot take your pet along, you can usually find someone who is willing to care for him for the few weeks of your vacation. We almost always have some guinea pig guests that our children's friends leave with us, and when we travel, my parents take care of our pets. During the day, the guinea pigs are in a run on the lawn, and at night they sleep in a cage indoors. Whenever you give your guinea pig to friends or relatives to keep, be sure to provide sufficient grains, hay, and litter. Also, leave some money for buying carrots, lettuce, and other fresh foods.

Pet Hotels

There are *pet hotels* and *pet stores* that will care for just about any pet during your absence. Make a reservation early because space is usually limited. At most pet stores you will have to deliver your guinea pig in his own cage. Pet hotels will often pro-

vide their own cages. Prices vary considerably, and it pays to.check with a number of places if you have a wide choice. You need not bring feeds as a rule unless you want your pet to have some special food. In most places the animals are well fed and kept very clean, and often a veterinarian makes regular visits.

Guinea Pig Families

A Couple Living Together

It is fun and interesting to keep a pair of guinea pigs. A pair does not take up much more space than a single animal, and if you keep a male and female, you will be able to observe their courting, mating, birthing, and parenting with an immediacy that is hardly possible with any other animal. Of course, you will have more work, too, because the raising of young guinea pigs requires much attention and care. You should be fully aware of that before you decide to keep a pair.

Male and female guinea pigs get along well together as a rule, although there can be differences of opinion from time to time, just as there are in all families. Two females living together will experience similar differences. These conflicts are reflected in a minor combativeness in which the teeth come into play but rarely in any serious way. Occasionally, one partner will pull some hair from the other's neck; and as a rule, it is the female that does this to show the male she has a will of her own or to ward off his overly ardent efforts at courtship. The male is always chivalrous toward the female. He will willingly leave to the female particularly tasty morsels that two males or two females would fight over bitterly.

Courting and Mating

The guinea pig husband is always very polite, considerate, and gentle toward his wife and always eager to stay in her favor. Every day he circles the female with slow, measured steps, shifting his weight from one hind foot to the other, and he sidles up to the female repeatedly, touching her body gently with his and "talking" to her in humming, chattering sounds. Until the animals come to know each other well, the female will resist the male's

Guinea pigs determine by scent whether they will get along together or not.

advances. She does this in a way that looks much more ferocious than it actually is. She sits up on her hind legs, stretches out her front legs, and—with wide open mouth—shows

Guinea Pig Families

the male her teeth. If this warning does not suffice, she will swat the male on the nose, whereupon he will retreat, squeaking his dismay. If a pair is well acquainted, the female will calmly avoid the male's approaches and occasionally shower him with a warning spray of urine. This usually keeps him in his place for quite some time.

The female comes into heat every fourteen to eighteen days. The eggs that have been developing in the female's ovaries are now ready to be fertilized. The vagina, which is normally closed off by a mucous plug, is now open for twenty-four hours; and now, after the courtship described above, the female is ready to accept the male. The female flattens herself on her belly and lifts up her hindquarters. The penis of the male enters the vagina and deposits the sperm needed to fertilize the eggs. The mating act lasts only a few seconds. Then both animals clean themselves thoroughly, particularly the genital area.

Pregnancy

After mating, the guinea pigs return to their normal pattern of behavior. Pregnancy lasts for about nine to ten weeks. I have seen litters of five or six young born after sixty days and litters of two or even one after as long as seventy-two days. The average litter has two to four young, which are born after a gestation period of sixty-five to sixty-eight days. After four or five weeks of pregnancy the female (sow) will get plumper and rounder. In the last two weeks of pregnancy, she becomes downright rotund. This is not surprising if you consider that the young often weigh more than half of the sow's own body weight. You can see and feel the movement of the young inside the womb when you are holding the sow on your lap or in your arms. Unlike a rabbit mother, the guinea pig sow makes no attempts at building a nest for her newborn, nor are there any other changes whatever in her behavior. She does not even chase the male out of the sleeping box.

Can the Father Attend the Birth?

With most rodents, the father cannot be present at the birth; but with guinea pigs, the female tolerates his presence quite well. Indeed, it seems to have a calming influence on the sow, and when I have sometimes removed the male or he has left the cage himself, the female objects to this abandonment by squeaking. The father usually displays no particular interest in the birth and retires quietly

Guinea Pig Families

to the far end of the cage. Only once have I seen a male guinea pig help lick the newborn dry. Thus, it is not necessary to remove the father before the young are due. But there is a reason why you may want to remove him anyhow. Only a few hours after parturition, the female comes into heat again and will accept the male for another mating. To prevent another pregnancy, you should separate the male and female, preferably a few days before the birth is expected.

A guinea pig mother is always intent on cleanliness and carefully licks her young from head to toe.

The Birth of the Young

The big day has finally come. The young are born. If you are lucky you can watch the birth if, as is usually the case, the birth occurs during the day. The mother will not object to your presence, and if you have children, you should let them watch the birth. My children always awaited the birth with great excitement and ran to the cage first thing every morning. How many young would there be? What would they look like? The children's patience was often sorely tried. But then they were sometimes surprised by a birth that came earlier than expected.

Weight at Birth and Litter Size

You will be amazed to see how big and well-developed the newborn babies are. We have always weighed the young on their birthday. The litters ranged from two to five young, and the smallest from a litter of five weighed 2 ounces (60 g). The larger in a litter of two weighed 4½ ounces (128 g). Some books quote birth weights as ranging from 1½ to 3½ ounces (40–100 g).

The Delivery

The delivery goes quickly and easily despite the large size of the newborn. Depending on the litter size, the delivery takes from ten to thirty minutes. We are always amazed to see how thoroughly in charge the new mother is. No sooner is the young animal born than the mother tears off the enveloping membrane and eats it. This is, of course, extremely important because the newborn would quickly suffocate if the membrane were not removed right after birth. Then the mother licks the baby's nose, eyes, and mouth to remove any fluid residues.

Guinea Pig Families

As soon as one baby is taken care of the next one appears. Only once did the babies — and then the mother — become spattered with blood. Usually there is some blood at the end of the delivery when the placenta is passed. The mother will eat some or all of the placenta. Let her do this, and remove anything she has left only later. During delivery, the mother is usually seated and receives the pup under her. With the newborn placed between her front legs, she tears off the membrane and licks the young clean.

Independent at Birth

Shortly after they are born, the young start looking around curiously at their world. Their eyes are open two weeks before birth, a fact confirmed by Caesarian sections and premature births. The young also have a fully developed coat, which glistens like silk as soon as the mother has licked it dry. Other interesting facts you will observe are that the newborn can walk immediately and can eat hay and other solid food right after birth. Their permanent teeth come in while they are still in the womb.

There are many advantages to the long gestation period. In the South American Andes, where clans of wild guinea pigs live together in dens and thickets and develop elaborate systems of paths, the young are ready at birth to run and to hide from their enemies. They are so independent that they can even get along without their mother, although they ordinarily nurse for about three weeks. This arrangement is much better for guinea pigs because their hiding places in the brush and in dens are not secure enough for blind, naked, and helpless young. To keep young of this kind safe, the wild rabbit, for example, has to dig long complicated burrows. Since the guinea pig is not equipped to do this but relies instead on its speed and agility and on the labyrinthine nature of its paths for safety, this long pregnancy and this independence of the young at birth are crucial to the survival of the species.

The Guinea Pig's Nursery

Guinea pig families live together in close but relaxed intimacy. The mother nurses her young frequently. She does this sitting up rather than lying on her side as most other animals do. She has only two teats, which are located well back on her belly. When the young nurse, they sit on either side of the mother and facing her. This sitting position while nursing is also a holdover from the wild where the guinea pig always has to be ready to run. Since the young can eat a lot of solid food a few days after birth, there is little squabbling, even in a large litter, over whose turn it is to drink. The young wait calmly for their turn, and each one gets a turn. After about three weeks, the mother goes dry, and the young lose interest in nursing. At three to five weeks of age, they can be separated from their mother. If there is limited space, as in an upstairs apartment, separation becomes mandatory at this age. Young females can be sexually mature at the early age of five to eight weeks, and young males are ready to mate at nine to ten weeks. At four to six months they will probably be parents themselves. If you want to avoid a growing guinea pig population, you will have to separate young animals into groups of males and females. This is unproblematic with the females, but the males will start fighting as they mature.

Young animals like to climb and jump, and a guinea pig hutch should be equipped with obstacles for this purpose.

The guinea pig's closely knit family life can be observed during the young animals' first days and weeks. You will see how the family does everything as a group. The children will follow both the father and the mother. If your animals run free in your house, it can happen that one of the babies will get separated from the others. You will immediately hear it squeaking "I'm lost," and just as quickly the mother will come. The two animals will sniff at each other, rub noses, and nudge each other. Then, with a kind of clucking, gurgling sound, the mother will lead the stray back to its littermates. The little ones often lie cuddled up together. Then they will run off one after another, in one door of the sleeping box and out the other. These little creatures are so agile and quick, are such daring gymnasts, and clear hurdles so easily that it is a sheer delight to watch them. Unfortunately, this playfulness declines in adulthood. However, it can be preserved to a considerable extent if you see to it that your animals stay fit and trim. You can do this by not overfeeding them and by giving them a lot of exercise running about in your house and yard.

Breeding Guinea Pigs

Prerequisites for Breeding

If you want to breed guinea pigs on a larger scale than just a litter or two now and then, very different conditions will have to be met. First and foremost comes the question of space. One pair with occasional offspring can be reasonably kept in an apartment, but an apartment simply cannot accommodate several pairs and their frequent litters. Hygiene becomes difficult, and even with the greatest care, some odor cannot be avoided. Breeding can be done in dry, well-ventilated basements, attics, sheds, or stables. In the summer, your animals can breed outdoors in your yard as long as they have a secure run and weather-tight housing.

The most important requirements for guinea pig breeders are reliability, punctuality, and love for the animals. A garden enables you to give your animals a varied diet, and it also helps keep costs down. In the summer you can give your guinea pigs fresh grass, or you can make hay, and your garden can produce winter feed in the form of carrots, turnips, cabbage, Jerusalem artichokes, and potatoes.

Different Breeding Methods

There are several approaches to breeding guinea pigs. If you are planning to breed for show or for specific genetic characteristics of color or fur you will have to attend carefully to details of breed selection and control. This calls for pair breeding and carefully kept records.

Pair Breeding

A hutch or cage for a breeder pair should have a floor area of at least 2 by 3 feet (80 × 60 cm) and be at least 14 to 15 inches (35–40 cm) high. If you do not stack your cages, you can use boxes without covers. While wood is a suitable material for most breeders, plastic or metal boxes or disposable cartons make cleaning and sanitation easier. If you do use wooden hutches, the front doors should be covered with wire mesh, as in rabbit hutches. Commercially available guinea pig boxes made of plastic are best (page 19). They are not as heavy as wooden cages. Also, they are easily washable, are open on top, and have a plexiglass front that makes it easy to see each animal clearly. These boxes can be kept alongside and one above the other on shelves. Their light weight lets you move them around easily without having to take the animals out. Another great advantage is ease in cleaning. It is a good idea to have more boxes than you have pairs. This way, you can put animals into clean yet familiar boxes while you clean and air dirty boxes. With this rotation system, you can go through all your boxes with relative ease and minimal disturbance to the animals.

Harem Breeding

Pair breeding is the most appropriate method for a breeder who has specific breeding goals in mind, such as developing new colors; but for breeders who want to produce large numbers of animals for supplying pet stores or research laboratories, harem breeding is better. This method brings several females (5, 10, or even as many as 20) together with a single male. For this method, you need larger breeding hutches. The following floor areas are required:

For 5 females with one male: 9 square feet (1 m²).

For 10 females with one male: 18 square feet (2 m²).

For 20 females with one male: 36 square feet (4 m²).

This allows each female and her young a little less than 2 square feet (0.2 m²), which is quite adequate because the large communal space is available to all the animals. With this method, the animals are kept in bays with concrete floors. The guinea pigs live raised above the concrete on wooden slats that let urine and droppings fall to the floor underneath. The wood has to be treated to keep it from rotting prematurely. Sawdust is the litter most often used beneath the slats, and it is changed as often as is necessary. A layer of straw on top of the slats is a good idea, but many breeders do without it. The concrete floor is sloped toward a drain to facilitate the washing and disinfection process.

The most suitable materials for the breeding of large numbers of guinea pigs are stainless steel and plastic. The materials should be able to withstand disinfection by strong chemicals and heat and should be seamless to prevent injuries to the animals as well as build-ups of dirt.

Choosing Breeder Stock

If you want to start breeding guinea pigs, you should buy animals between two and four months old. These animals are smaller than full-grown adults and will weigh ten to twenty ounces (300–600 g). They can and should be bred at this age. With older animals there is the risk that females will not conceive easily or will not conceive at all. Complications occur most often with fully grown animals. Older females that have never had a litter or have not had one for a long time are prone to premature births and still births or sometimes cannot deliver their young naturally. They will die a painful death if they are not delivered by Caesarian section. It is very hard to judge the age of an adult

Breeding Guinea Pigs

guinea pig. The inexperienced buyer may well wind up with a five or six-year-old animal that has been culled from breeding stock. You will not be able to get far in breeding with a female like that. Here are some signs that will help you recognize an old animal: The fur is no longer smooth and shiny; the ears, which have very little hair on them in any animal, will be almost bare in an old animal; and the skin on and around the ears will be leathery.

The male that will sire large numbers of offspring should be of top quality and have outstanding breed characteristics. He must be strongly built, have a good growth rate, and show excellent coloring and hair density. The quality of the young will depend just as much on the mother, too, of course; and this is why both parents should be chosen with great care.

Breeder females can be bred for about four years. Males can often be used one year longer. Even then their fertility is only reduced, not lost. For the large-scale breeder, however, such animals are no longer economical, and he will sell them. The amateur breeder will have become attached to his old animals, though, and will lavish even more tender care on them precisely because they are old.

Breeder Associations

In Europe, guinea pigs are bred and shown mainly in Holland and England where standards for certain breeds have been developed. There are many established breeds, and shows where prize animals are selected are held every year.

In the United States the most common strains are the "No. 2 and 13" and the "Dunkin-Hartley" strain. These are white strains used mostly in research and kept by pet owners who do not show their animals. Guinea pig fanciers and their associations favor the Angoras (called "Shelties" in Britain) and the Peruvian breeds, which have very long and rough coats. There are also the "Fuzzy" and "Star" strains and many color variations.

Guinea Pig Breeds

Smooth-Haired Breeds

The coat of smooth-haired guinea pig breeds resembles that of their cousins in the wild. The first Europeans to come to South America found not only solid-colored guinea pigs but also checked strains. *Brown and white checked* and *solid white* animals were widespread at that time, but *black* and *black and white checks* were still unknown.

Agouti Guinea Pigs

Of the smooth-haired breeds, the *Agouti* guinea pigs resemble their wild ancestors most in their coloring. The name was derived from a South American rodent that is only a distant relative of the guinea pig and belongs to the subfamily Dasyproctinea. The agouti is larger and has longer legs than the guinea pig. Substrains are the golden agouti and the black agouti, and because there is a guinea pig breed with a similar reddish brown coloration, it is called the *Gold Agouti*. The *Silver Agouti* is whitish gray. A third substrain is called the *Wild Agouti* because its gray-brown fur resembles that of the wild cavy. The coat of Agouti guinea pigs has four color zones. The hair tips are black; next comes a gray-brown, red-brown, or whitish zone; below that is another almost black zone; and next to the skin the hair is cream colored. These various color zones create a characteristic "ticking" or salt-and-pepper effect. There should not be any distinct stripes or spots.

The Self or Solid-Colored Guinea Pigs

Self guinea pigs are bred in seven colors: *black, chocolate, red, lilac, beige, cream,* and *white.* The color should be strong and evenly distributed over the body. Solid-colored guinea pigs are usually stocky in build.

Albino Guinea Pigs

These popular and attractive animals are pure white with red eyes, but they have dark flecks on the nose, ears, and feet. These typical dark markings are familiar to us from Siamese cats and Russian rabbits. They are known as "cold spots" because newborn animals do not have them and they are most marked in older animals that have been exposed to cold weather.

Himalayan Guinea Pigs

This breed resembles the Albino, but along with its black nose, ears, and feet, it has black eyes. These guinea pigs are popular as pets and are widely used in research laboratories.

Dutch Guinea Pigs

The basic color of the Dutch guinea pig is white, but it may also have very specific markings in black, chocolate, red, gold agouti, or silver agouti. The colors have to be located on the cheeks, ears, hind legs, and hindquarters, and they have to be sharply set off from the white background. The name of this breed was taken from the Dutch rabbit.

English Tortoiseshell-and-White or Checked Guinea Pigs

Good representatives of this strain are tricolored in red, white, and black, and the colors are distributed in square checks on either side of a center line down the back. The standards here call for three colors. This checked strain is the most popular for house pets. Even if an animal's coloring and color pattern are not up to show standards, it may still make a highly attractive and charming pet.

Tortoiseshell Guinea Pigs

This strain shows the same checked pattern as the Tortoiseshell-and-White, but in this strain there are only two colors—red and black—instead of three. Animals with the smallest, most evenly distributed checks of color are the most valuable show animals.

Long-Haired Breeds

Abyssinian Guinea Pigs

These guinea pigs are bred in all the colors and color combinations we have seen in the smooth-haired breeds.

However, their coats are longer and rougher than those of the smooth-haired breeds. Their most striking characteristic is the pattern of rosettes or whorls that their rough coats form.

Angora Guinea Pigs

The long-haired breeds generally known as Angora guinea pigs are very beautiful, but their long coats require a great deal of care. They, too, can be bred in all of the previously mentioned colors and color combinations. There are two main long-haired types: The body hair of the *Angora* grows to about six inches (15 cm) in length, but the hair on the head remains short. In the *Peruvian* guinea pig the hair on both body and head is long, and it is often difficult to tell at a glance which end of the animal is which. The longer the hair the more valuable the animal is. If you want to breed Angoras you will have to be careful to maintain genetic purity over many generations.

Understanding Guinea Pigs

Sounds, Body Language, and Behavior

Guinea pigs can produce a wide variety of sounds. They can squeak, squeal, chatter, growl, purr, and grunt. But they do not whistle as is often claimed.

Summoning a Companion

What may sound like a whistle is in fact a loud, high squeak that the guinea pig uses to summon either one of his own kind or his trusted caretaker. Maja, an attractive, tricolored female we kept as our only guinea pig for several years, developed such a close tie to the children and me that every time we entered our apartment she greeted us with loud squeaks. This she did faithfully even though she was kept in my study a good thirty feet (10 m) away from the front door and separated from us by the door to the study. In the evenings, when I went out to send off my mail, I had gotten into the habit of bringing back some grass or dandelion greens for Maja. As soon as my key was in the lock, she would call out with a particularly long, high squeak.

I sometimes tried to outwit Maja by sneaking into the house as quietly as I could, but I never succeeded. Her hearing was so keen that she could recognize my children's footsteps coming up the stairs and could even distinguish them from other people's.

I often observed how she would stand up on her hind legs and look toward the door just before the children rang the doorbell. She was always interested in their arrival because they, too, usually picked some greens for her on their way home from school. Our other guinea pigs squeaked less frequently than Maja, but when they did, they, too, wanted attention.

Young guinea pigs emit loud, pathetic squeaks if they find themselves too far away from their mother. She responds by coming to them immediately and soothing them with a kind of cooing, murmuring sound. The two animals sniff each other, then the mother licks her baby's face.

Establishing Rank

Whenever two guinea pigs that do not know each other meet, they circle each other slowly, hiss and snap their

Typical stance for intimidating strange animals. When guinea pigs first meet, they circle each other on fully extended legs.

60

teeth together, raise their backs, and come at each other stiff-leggedly. Each tries to outflank the other and bite him in the neck or nose. But these encounters do not inevitably end in biting. More often than not this performance has the purpose of impressing the stranger. Even guinea pig females that know each other will indulge in this kind of mock battle. However, peace soon reigns again. This is not the case among males. The loser in the battle for rank will continue to be attacked and chased away. There is no room in a guinea pig clan for two adult males. A strong male will establish himself as a pasha who rules the harem. The young males form their own groups on the fringes of the clan. When they are full grown, they will try to attract females and start their own families.

Courtship

When a male guinea pig approaches a female, he makes a kind of humming, chattering sound. He will circle the female, swaying back and forth from side to side. He will also drive her ahead of him and spray her with urine.

Communication

Guinea pigs are very social animals and do everything together. They have a great deal to say to each other and in the course of most of their activities, they communicate with gurgling sounds. These sounds soothe, reassure, and create contact. Whenever guinea pigs move through tall grass where they cannot keep each other in sight all the time, these sounds help maintain group unity. This comforting gurgling reassures each member that all is well and no danger threatens.

Unity in the Clan

A guinea pig clan keeps in touch not only by sound but also by sight and scent. The animals walk in single file, and the young are usually placed between the adult members of the pack. With this marching order, wild guinea pigs establish beaten paths crisscrossing their territory.

Sensory Capacities and the Ability to Learn

Sight

Guinea pigs have a keen sense of sight. Their peripheral vision is especially well developed, and they can readily spot enemies approaching from in front of them, from either side, and from above. Although golden hamsters, mice, rats and some other rodents cannot distinguish colors, guinea pigs can recognize all the colors of the spectrum, particularly the primary colors, yellow, red, and blue, but also the secondaries orange, violet, and green.

The Ability to Distinguish Colors

We conducted our own experiments to test guinea pigs' ability to distinguish colors and their capacity to learn. We placed plastic bowls of the same size but in a variety of colors — red, yellow, green, and blue — about two feet (60 cm) apart. We filled the red bowl with grain but left the others

Guinea pigs can distinguish colors and learn to recognize a bowl with food in it by its color and markings.

empty. To be sure the animals did not rely on their sense of smell to find the correct bowl, we left all the bowls filled with the same food until just before our test. Then we emptied all but the red bowl and let the hungry guinea pig run toward the bowls from the other side of the room. At first, of course, he ran from one bowl to another until he found the full one. We took the animal back to the start-

ing point and let him look for the food again. Our most intelligent guinea pig needed fourteen tries before he learned to go straight to the red bowl. He was not confused if we laid the bowls out in a different order; but when we put the food in the green instead of the red bowl, all our animals had trouble assimilating this change, but they did eventually "crack" the new code.

Hearing

The guinea pig's hearing is, if anything, keener than its vision. It can detect high frequencies that lie far beyond the range of the human ear. When we are young, we can hear frequencies up to 20,000 Hz. Adults at thirty-five years of age can hear no more than 15,000 Hz. Guinea pigs, however, can hear sounds up to 30,000 Hz. The lower limit for both humans and guinea pigs lies around 16 Hz. We can just barely hear the low, rumbling sound guinea pigs make.

How much guinea pigs rely on their sense of hearing is shown by the fact that they have developed such a highly sophisticated "language." Also, they react most promptly to acoustic stimuli. If another guinea pig emits screams of fear or pain, all the others run and hide in a safe place or race around their cage in panic. The mother of a guinea pig will not respond when she sees one of her young

in a dangerous situation, but she will come immediately if one of her young signals by squeaking that he is lost.

Guinea pigs quickly learn to respond to a specific sound. If you reward them every time with a piece of carrot or some other treat, they will soon learn to come when you call their names, whistle in a certain way, or ring a bell.

Sense of Smell

The guinea pig's sense of smell is also highly developed. It is not as keen as a dog's, but it is still far superior to ours. A guinea pig is able to distinguish concentrations of scent 100 to 1,000 times smaller than we can and to recognize every other animal in his clan by its scent. The guinea pig also identifies familiar humans by scent.

Touch

The long tactile whiskers of a guinea pig serve the same function as they do in cats, enabling the animal to navigate safely in dim light or thick underbrush.

Feeding Behavior

The feeding habits of guinea pigs differ from those of mice, hamsters, and squirrels. They do not carry food to their mouths with their forepaws. Instead they put their front feet on a lettuce leaf, corncob, or apple to hold it still (see figure on page 13). If we hold food up above their heads, they will rise up on their hind legs to reach for it. But this is always a brief and unsteady movement because guinea pigs cannot sit on their thighs. They can only balance on their hind feet.

Learning through Play

Young guinea pigs up to the age of four months love to jump. When we had young animals we put a partition in their cage that had openings in it about four to six inches up from the floor. Several times a day the young animals played running and climbing games, racing around in circles and jumping through the holes in the partition with great glee. My children have often used large wooden blocks to build a labyrinth with hurdles and hiding places in it. It was a real pleasure to see how eagerly and agilely the animals scurried through this maze. Sometimes even the older animals took a few turns.

Offer Your Pet Some Challenges

It is important that your guinea pig's native capacities and instincts be challenged. Do not let your animal just vegetate in his cage. Proper care means giving him something to do as well as providing him with food and shelter. He has to have a chance to exercise his physical and mental abilities and stay fit. A guinea pig that is lively and adventurous is a much more interesting animal for you and your child than one that sits quietly in his cage and has no reason for existing except to be petted occasionally. Make use of the suggestions I have made in this chapter. I know from my own personal experience that they will keep your guinea pig active, healthy, and happy.

Books for Further Information

The Biology of the Guinea Pig
J. Wagner and P. Manning,
eds.: Academic Press

Breeding Guinea Pigs
Jennifer Axelrod: TFH Publications

Index

Index

Perfect for Pet Owners!

"Clear, concise...written in simple, nontechnical language."

—Booklist

'A solid bet for first-time pet owners"
—Booklist

We've taken all the best features of our popular Pet Owner's Manuals and added *more* expert advice, *more* sparkling color photographs, *more* fascinating behavioral insights, and fact-filled profiles on the leading breeds. Indispensable references for pet owners, ideal for people who want to compare breeds before choosing a pet. Over 120 illustrations per book — 55 to 60 in full color!

"Stunning"
—Roger Caras
Pets & Wildlife

THE NEW AQUARIUM HANDBOOK Scheurmann (3682-4)
THE NEW BIRD HANDBOOK Vriends (4157-7)
THE NEW CAT HANDBOOK Ulrike Müller (2922-4)
THE NEW DOG HANDBOOK H.J. Ullmann (2857-0)
THE NEW DUCK HANDBOOK Raethel (4088-0)
THE NEW FINCH HANDBOOK Christa Koepf (2859-7)
THE NEW GOAT HANDBOOK Jaudas (4090-2)
THE NEW PARAKEET HANDBOOK Birmelin/Wolter (2985-2)
THE NEW PARROT HANDBOOK Lantermann (3729-4)
THE NEW SOFTBILL HANDBOOK W. Steinigeweg (4075-9)
THE NEW TERRIER HANDBOOK Kerry Kern (3951-3)

BARRON'S 250 Wireless Boulevard, Hauppauge, NY 11788